Hidden Things

poems

HIDDEN THINGS (c) 2024 E.S. Cuny III
All Rights Reserved

No part of this book may be used or reproduced in any manner whatsoever without permission except in the case of brief quotations embodied in critical essays or reviews.

This is a work of the poet's iumadination. Any references to historical events, real people, or real places are used fictitiously. Other names, characters, places, and events are products of the author's imagination, and any resemblance to actual events or places or persons, living or dead, is entirely coincidental.

Attention schools and businesses; for discounted copies on large orders please contact the publisher directly.

Kallisto Gaia Press Inc.
PO Box 220
Davilla TX 76523
info@kallistogaiapress.org
(254) 654-7205

Front Cover photo: *Unknown Subject* by E. S. Cuny III
Poet's Photo: Alex Labrey
Cover Design: E. S. Cuny III

ISBN: 978-1-952224-42-3

Distributed by Ingram Lightning Source

Library of Congress control info available on request.

Hidden Things

poems

E.S. Cuny III

Other Works by E.S. Cuny III

Poetry Chap Books

These Are Good Poems!
Halloween, Fireside or Just Plain Weird Poems
A Floe of Life
Rated "R"
(The Poetic Reminisces of a Recalcitrant and Unrepentant Roue)

One Act Plays

Guy Lussac, Last King of the Yardmen
Red Canyon; or, To Mars and Back with Chili Mac

Contest Shorts

Lost Night at the Armadillo
Nero the Wolf
The Mermaid Bar and Grill
Case 146

TABLE OF CONTENTS

The Hidden Pool	1
November Rains	2
This Old House	3
Reality Behind the Curtain	4
Blankets	6
Radiation Daze	7
Pills Glorious Pills	8
How To Get To Sleep	9
In Bun Hair	11
The Ways of Things	12
Just a Sheet of Paper	13
Remembering Huff	15
Be Original!	16
Jigsaws	17
Bus Balloons	18
Coming Into Nairo	19

To my friends, hidden treasures all.

*There is more poetry
in one cat's curl than all the
verses in the world.*

-- Attributed to Sir Scarfy T.C.

The Hidden Pool

Come,
take my hand
run with me and jump –
into the rocky pool of time.

Watch,
as waves ripple out
returning faint images
obscured in fractal rhyme.

Grasp,
at meanings just beyond reach,
from a future shore's
far and distant line.

Then
dance, dance, dance
to a spectral music
that is but silence sublime.

Wake up!
Daylight calls to sunlit walls
forget all you have ever seen –
until one day you experience
that person, place, event or thing
vaguely remembered from a dream.

November Rains

I'm standing in November rain, waiting for a delivery.
Not aimlessly mind you, I got the message.
The dog is sniffing around, impatient. And me too.
Even though I've been too far to know, one package
won't completely, immediately change my life
       (But this one might?)

I pull the old collar tighter, shift my feet under the tree
dodging drops, dog anxious wondering why we stopped,
wants to leave. But I know what's coming. And maybe,
just maybe, it will be the one. We wait for the truck
       at the corner of Liberty and Texas.

She asked for two sources before handing it over.
I know it won't be exactly what I wanted. (And it cost
more than I thought.) I want to rip the wrapping off – now!
But no, the wait is somehow tender. I can hear you.
       Wait.

Padding over the floor, tape and packing paper
strewn about, an empty cardboard box,
torn ribbon; an old friend and new expectations,
       unfolded into one.

This Old House

The back door banged shut all summer long
until the rains of autumn came pouring down.
Then windows that were stuck, opened up,
the door's angle shifted, closing without a sound.

The house will stay that way for awhile
until next season's weather roils right in,
riding along on the earthen swells, the walls
will expand and contract again and again.

This is the way the house breathes, sustaining
a life on a timeline beyond our comprehension.
Over the years of changes the house resets itself
constantly creaking while changing position.

As inhabitants move out and on, the house remains
and sometimes sighs as any other living breathing thing.

Reality Behind the Curtain

I.

When I grew up, headlines said God was no more,
and I thought *finally* we can get on with our lives,
and get away from all this overbearing religious
intrusion and so many pulpits so full of lies.
    I was so naïve.

I knew Our Generation would coalesce like no other.
We demanded an end to an illegal war overseas,
demanded truth from our up-tight government,
and we marched together for a world in peace.
    I was so naïve.

Oh yes we were marching, for rights and equality
and we were bound together in Rock & Roll.
We wouldn't need mortgages, or ego-politicians.
Heck, we weren't going to trust anyone 30 or more.
    I was so naïve.

And America was a great country, that other nations
looked up to and sought for opportunity and justice.
Yeah, we had veered off track but we could put it back
and find a way to once again regain our original purpose.

After all if you just ran things in a way that was rational
then we could still believe our country was exceptional …
    Dear God, I was *so* naïve.

II.

And yet, and yet the spark is still there not to give in to despair,
and have faith in the strength of that founding resolution,
that brought an idea of enlightenment for society's betterment
into reality, through the document of the American constitution.

It's an instrument that is under constant attack
from without and within each and every day
but for belief in its process I will gladly embrace
      any remaining naivete.

Blankets

Towels are draped from the balconies of water-front localities,
    some orange some purple some green.
Some with patterns some with images and sometimes even
    yellow bikinis and denim blue jeans,
giving all kinds of testaments to multi-cultural sentiments
    and of the personalities inside unseen.

In the southwest are roadside stands that families set up
    and string out lines from pick-up trucks,
to hang a 'For Sale' sign on handmade blankets and rugs.
    Extraordinary designs sway in the breeze
over laden tables of turquoise jewelry and hand made mugs;
    but oh! the wondrous incredible weaves.

Along county road Number Nine fence posts hold a hog wire line,
    between the poles are perfect places
in dewy morning light to catch the sight of spider webs' designs.
    Silvery spirals shine in a pulsating breeze
showing no match between each batch of intervening spaces;
    each pattern made according to breed.

When I look up at night at the starry sight I know out there
    galaxies are spiraling across the sky.
No two are the same, dark or aflame, each a beauty beyond compare.
    The vastness of infinity seems quietly benign
yet somewhere within lies a magical whim, that deeply innate
    overwhelmingly universal compulsion to create.

Radiation Daze

First were normal outside clarifications
from teeth to feet and even an x-rayed knee.
But three letters of warning brought full explorations
so they took shots at everything else in-between.
Then they got serious and turned it into a weapon,
which required paper-work to do by the ream.

It was hard to tell if anything had happened
when first I was put under the high power beam.
Experiences are often shared by other patients,
from "it won't hurt at all", to "when you pee you'll scream."
The whole situation required a modicum of patience
from us, the aimers, the calibraters – the whole damn team.

Now even though it's 'sposed to be over
administrations and medicines still continue,
the taking of blood goes on for now and forever
to monitor the killing of that which is in you,
in an effort to metamorphisize a nightmare's haunts;
yet in the background of dreams, still it taunts.

Pills Glorious Pills

Pills, glorious pills
good for whatever ills-ya,
they might even heals-ya,
unless they kills-ya.
Those pills
      glorious pills.

Pills glorious pills
You take 'em by the handful
you take 'em by the jar full
even if they're awful.
Who cares what they are
just stick to a schedule
or else you might find
      you've taken 'em too far.

Pills glorious pills
They can make your brain be better
they can give you faster feet,
take away your anxiety
wake you up or give you sleep.
Treat every organ inside you
and even your outer skin,
help you not get pregnant
or engage
      in a little sin.

And when you've got a mouthful
try and tell 'em you're grateful
for all the ones that thrills ya,
don't worry when they bills ya
for giving out those pills, ya
just take some other pills, ya,
no need to worry about those
      pills, glorious pills.

How To Get To Sleep

I.

Lay down, stretch out then wiggle the toes. Now –
      better fluff that pillow a little.
Okay relax the knees then – oops, better check
      the back door is locked.
 OK. Shut the eyes oh, better check all the are lights off
      then pull the shades,
it should be dark, after all. Now too hot? To cold? Better go
      check that thermostat.
Best to re-fluff the pillows. Now relax the face by
      wriggling the ears, nose and lips.
Is that the cat wanting out? Jeez, let him.
      OK, fold the hands together
was that a car door slam? Just take a peek.
      Now think of clouds and, wait –
go quick and drink a bit of water before going to bed.
      Fluff, wiggle, lay out, eyes
hands – did you take that pill? OK, breathe deep,
      what the heck is that dog barking at?
Sometimes it helps to count to twenty, slowly
      and not think about what
she said or what he didn't say – what does that mean?
      You don't need to think
 about that thing you got to do tomorrow
      or else they'll – wait,
it's morning but what was that dream?
      Can't quite grab it ...

II.

What happened to all those faces I once knew?
The mirrors grabbed them, shuttered their wings
and holding them tight, ran down the halls of night
to open in the morning in other places
and put on the people who'd grown into them.

In Bun Hair

The Ways of Things

I do believe things like to disappear a lot,
and I've found their biggest friend is gravity,
but they also love to jump around at night,
for them it's a matter of great frivolity.

They'll take turns deciding who gets to get lost
and scuttle about looking for places to hide.
Then they won't reappear again until
they chose to pop up in front of your eyes.

One trick is to get next to something similar
so when quickly looking, it's dismissed as a mirage.
Another ploy is hiding under paper or cloth
often quite effective as a kind of camouflage.

Your shoes will walk about in the dark
while you're sleeping they're having fun,
and in the morning you'll be really lucky
if at all you can find even one.

Keys or earrings or credit cards love to slip
into the gaps between cushions or behind shelves.
Wallets and phones have been known to get lost
with the help of giggling elves.

Wedding rings love to hop into sinks
and funnel down the drains.
And if nothing else, things can just 'disappear',
for the fun of befuddling your brain.

Yet it's easy enough to stop this stuff
and I'll let you know how, just as fast as
I can write it down – that is, once I've found
where I've left my glasses!

Just a Sheet of Paper

It was just a piece of paper, only a mere sheet
        blowing sideways up then down
flitting in and out of traffic, wafting down the street.

An unnoticed escapee from a rear window's slit
        now at the whim of the wind
soon to be forever lost, oh! What secrets are in it?

The driver ahead, in a one-way conversation,
        hasn't missed it yet
but might need it later for some presentation.

Maybe it's a type of legal decree
        wait, a hand is twirling –
ah-ha, the finish to the Unfinished Symphony?

Could it be the recipe for San Francisco cakes,
        directions to a new job,
perhaps Amelia's final last coordinates?

Or maybe a cue sheet for an audition,
        or address to a big date,
could be the big book deal's final decision?

Perhaps Fermat's original theorem's solution
        or Quantum Theory unified –
at last!, or the lost formula for cold fusion?

Instructions from IKEA, "No not that," I tremble,
        realizing that now
what ever it is will never be assembled.

The hand now is palm up and moving sideways
        obviously a sign of:
Irrefutable Proof who wrote Shakespeare's plays.

So many secrets to remain forever unknown
        slipping away unnoticed
with expressive gestures while on a cell phone.

Yet maybe these secrets give life some meaning
        when are best not known —
like the one about what happens after our final ending?

Remembering Huff

Every neighborhood has had its local poet, ours was
dearly beloved, slightly shabby, old Albert Huffstickler.
Not very famous by wealthy standards, who's verse
would rate fair to good if you're not much of a nitpicker.
 He would sit at the nearby bistro with his cigarettes, coffee
and pen, until the day his eyes gave up that final flicker.

He said he'd leave to me his rhyming machine
though it was left out of his will and trust.
But I found it later in a far back room
under a tarp and all covered with rust.
It still looked new, like it'd never been used
and I tried but it wouldn't start up.

So I wandered around his boxed up thoughts
looking for his 'Rhythmic Pentameters' book.
It was on top of a stack in the back marked 'Personal,'
but I figured it'd be all right if I took a look …
yet on pulling it out and opening it up
the pages were blank, then scattered amok.

Next I found a crate that was marked 'Oblivion'.
In order to open it I had to pry up its boards,
hoping to find his patterns of thought-composition.
But the pages turned into sand that spilled on the floor,
and squiggled into figures in the layers of dust,
forming mystic runes that spelled out, 'Long Live Huff.'

Be Original!

Ya wanna stick to the straight and narrow
so you put one foot in front of the other
then you can bootstrap up by sticking
a shoe in the door. Just tighten your belt,
it's a cinch, and buckle up 'cause,
just so you know it's not who you know
it's what you know!
        And be original.

It's a snap. Just cross your fingers then
it's just a slap on the wrist if you point it out.
But roll up your sleeves and get ready
to use some elbow grease, then put a chip
on your shoulder and keep a stiff neck
because remember, it's not what you know
it's who you know. Take my advice and,
        be original.

So square that jaw, keep your nose clean
and your eye on the ball, watch your P's and Q's,
then dot the I's and cross the T's.
and don't forget to say "Cheese". Be sure
to get the inside track 'cause what you'll need
is a friend at court. See, who knows
what you not that's you what know how?
Most of all, remember,
        be original!

Jigsaws

We set the table up and pull the old box down
open it up, turn it over and splay the parts around,
with lots of anticipation – and a little trepidation –
we marvel at the colors and the funny shapes we've found.

Some begin by sorting pieces, piling them up as if on a mission
searching for meaningful faces in facets weirdly misshapen.
Others seek out special lines, as those that have their edges straight
hoping a border will bring at least, a beginning of comprehension.

The puzzles can bring out many a fond reminiscence
reminding us of particular places and previous events,
such as rainy day cabins and old family gatherings.
Then into the task we dive, trying to make it make sense.

Hoping that this one here could almost fill a single's empty space,
only to connect with its perfect partner over in another place.
So many times things just don't fit, but doggedly we ply away at it,
past matches, mismatches and gaps until we begin to have a shape.

As the frame is nearly complete and the jaggedy picture appears
an anxiousness pervades the air, now we see the end is near.
Some contentedly stand aside – while others of us desperately try,
to put together the missing puzzle pieces of our lives.

Bus Balloons

It
can be
in a bus, or a car, or a
train; a cabin – or even a bar –
any enclosed space that has people within.
Someone argues with someone else; another one
talks on the phone. A joke is told to laughs and grins;
a boy smiles to a girl, she hums a song, he joins in, sings
along. "Hey, listen to this," sports fans turn a radio up.
Grandfathers pass babies photos around, aunties cluck
at their niece's evening gown, and as mothers compare
grocery prices, the chatter grows, their children make
faces and giggle, as a rooster crows(!). Sound levels
slowly rise, ballooning inside sheltering walls,
a cacophony that's almost palpable. These
jocular, independent lines of thought,
combining into one breathing
conversation
– until:

silence.

Sudden.
Absolute. Nothingness.
Pin-drop quiet. Aural abstinence
cached in surrounding sussuration,
hearing suspended in complete cessation.
As if everyone stopped at just the same time
to listen to everyone else; or everyone ran out
of things to say and sat looking with open mouths.
Then – a bump. A sneeze. Or something popped. Or
maybe something dropped. A passenger steps off
or gets on, or someone goes or someone comes.
Or a baby laughs or cries; then "Those groceries
keep going up"; "Did you see them in that?"
"Here take a look at this"; "Oh yes,
me too I have one too... See?"
And: all is alive, alive
again –
Ah!

Coming Into Nairo

Nairo lies that way, upon the Nile.
We shall not make encampment to-night.
No, we shall ride the remaining distance,
a long camel's run away, so they tell us.
No matter. I have been dazed all day
by the pyramids and how the sun burned
their after image into my eyes.
Surely the paint on them is made of gold.
I pick fleas from my hair as the guides
      urge greater speed.

Already the camels gallop. My heart beats fast.
Many of us have never been to the city before.
We wonder, will Keyops be a gracious lord?
I have been summoned to an audience before
Great Pharaoh. There I will beguile his court
with tales of the Dream-Poems I have had,
and surely then be appointed Royal Seer. Or perhaps
even better, Court Mentor to the Royal Daughter.
Failing that, Court Scribe-Poet? It all depends on
      those darn Dream-Poems.

But the guide's whip flicks against my side getting
my attention jostling my camel, nearly unseating me.
My man servant would have never allowed that, but
he has gone missing. The guides want more speed
and urge the camels faster. An anguished cry rises
far behind. Dreams be damned, I lash my camel
shouting, "Cush! Cush!" with the others as the guides
nervously point back into the dark, looking for
the eyes of the panthers and other winged creatures
      following us.

This writer hopes you've enjoyed these poetics and if so you may find more of his works on your favorite large e- commerce company. And if you wish to comment, question or simply communicate with the author e-mail him at: ifandorx9@gmail.com;
– Thank you.

www.ingramcontent.com/pod-product-compliance
Lightning Source LLC
Chambersburg PA
CBHW052128070526
44586CB00016B/2132